APOLO ANTON OHNO

Skating on the edge

Going for the
GOLD

APOLO ANTON OHNO
Skating on the edge

Thomas Lang

AVON BOOKS
An Imprint of HarperCollins Publishers

Produced by 17th Street Productions,
an Alloy, Inc. company
151 West 26th Street, New York, NY 10001

Library of Congress Catalog Card Number: 2002091349
ISBN 0-06-051843-X

First Avon edition, 2002

AVON TRADEMARK REG. U.S. PAT. OFF.
AND IN OTHER COUNTRIES,
MARCA REGISTRADA, HECHO EN U.S.A.

Visit us on the World Wide Web!
www.harperchildrens.com

To all future Olympic hopefuls

Contents

INTRODUCTION:

Mission Apolo

Salt Lake City, Utah. Closing ceremonies. The 2002 Olympic Games.

The greatest two weeks of Apolo Anton Ohno's life were coming to an end.

When he first arrived, people had high hopes for this nineteen-year-old, bandana-wearing, short track speed skater. He was the best in the world. Everyone across the United States was expecting medals. They were even calling these Olympics "Apolo's Games."

Apolo didn't disappoint.

Apolo treated the world to some of the most exciting competition in Olympic history. And he grabbed a gold and a silver medal while doing it. But it hadn't been easy. Short track speed skating is fast-paced, physical racing. Skaters cruise at thirty-five miles per hour only inches away from each other. People expected dramatic races with hair-raising finishes, and that's exactly what Apolo gave them. With all the crashes, disqualifications, and injuries, every race was a nail-biter. Every race took all Apolo had just to compete. Now it was coming to a close.

Apolo thought about what he had accomplished. He replayed the races in his mind as the closing ceremonies continued. He thought about the crashes, his injuries, the disqualifications. It had all been so crazy, so confusing. He could barely get his mind around what had happened there in Salt Lake. He was surrounded by nearly 2,500 athletes and 50,000 spectators. Millions more were watching on TV. Musicians like Christina Aguilera, Kiss, and *NSYNC jammed in the background. An endless stream of fireworks exploded overhead. People were dancing and cheering. Everyone was celebrating. It was an awesome sight. Still, for Apolo, nothing that night matched the excitement and frenzy of his competitions.

The races of the past two weeks were no different than his entire career had been. The whole six years of training that had led up to this point had been a wild ride. He had hung out with gangs, washed out of training programs, struggled with his father, been abandoned by his mother. Apolo had an incredible story—so incredible that when the Olympics started, people were already talking about it. And by the closing ceremonies—after Apolo had demonstrated that he was one of the best athletes in the world—his story was being told around the world.

What is Apolo's tale? Turn the page.

CHAPTER ONE:

From In-Lines to Ice Skates

So what's the childhood of an Olympic speed skater like? Well, it's probably a little different for everyone. Usually skaters grow up surrounded by their sport. Think of American speed skaters and you think of places like Wisconsin, North Dakota, and Minnesota—places where lakes and rivers can freeze for six months out of the year.

One of the last places you'd think a champion speed skater would grow up would be Seattle. It's rainy, not too cold, and right by the ocean. There's not much snow and hardly ever any ice. Seattle just isn't a place where people spend a lot of time skating. All the same, this mild, wet city by the sea is the hometown of the most famous speed skater in the U.S.: a nineteen-year-old kid with an earring and long hair, named Apolo Ohno.

How did Seattle become home to the 2002 Olympics' most exciting speed skater?

Apolo Anton Ohno was born in Seattle on May 22, 1982. Back then no one was counting on an Olympic future for this kid. Things were pretty tough on him right off the bat. His mother, Jerrie Lee, abandoned him in 1983 before he was even one year old. After she took off, he never heard from her again.

Apolo's father, Yuki Ohno, was left to raise Apolo as a single dad. It wasn't easy, but he managed as well as he could. Mr. Ohno was a hairstylist in Seattle and worked like crazy to keep up with the bills. He owned his own hair salon called Yuki's Diffusions, which took up a lot of his time. And he sometimes took on extra jobs at other salons just to make ends meet. He often worked twelve-hour days. Juggling his time before his son was born had been hard enough. After Apolo arrived and his wife left, things got even crazier.

"It was a turning point in my life," Mr. Ohno says, describing the early years, after his wife left. "I was the type of hairdresser that goes to parties and all those shows wearing very flamboyant European label suits from head to toe. Everything changed. At the beginning I felt I had no confidence. I thought, I'm the only male caring for a one-year-old baby, facing all the other mothers and day care. I was very depressed. But you just develop. You build up confidence."

Another thing that made things difficult was Apolo's personality. No one had any idea that Apolo would be skating in the Olympics. But as soon as he could walk, Apolo definitely demonstrated that he had the soul of an athlete and a competitor. He would jump the fence at day care, climb to the top of the jungle gym and refuse to come down, and even swallow dirt and rocks on dares. Basically, he had a rambunctious and uncontrollable kind of energy—the kind of energy that makes Olympic champions but that also makes for hard-to-manage kids. Chasing after Apolo was a full-time job, and it was almost impossible for Mr. Ohno just to make dinner or take Apolo shopping at the grocery store. It was exhausting and often sent Mr. Ohno into fits of panic and worry.

But even when Apolo was young, his wild spirit was no mystery to Mr. Ohno. He knew exactly where it came from. He'd been something of a rebel himself.

Mr. Ohno was born in Japan and was the son of a vice-president of a Japanese university. At eighteen, Mr. Ohno decided to leave his academic family and his unexciting life in Japan to try his luck in the U.S. He moved to Seattle, where he enrolled at Seattle City College. He wanted to be an accountant. But after a few courses in accounting, he decided that wasn't for him either—too many numbers, not enough socializing. Instead, he decided to check out another career.

Mr. Ohno studied hairstyling and traveled all over the world to learn his craft. He went to London to study at the famous Vidal Sassoon salon and spent time in New York City practicing his trade. He partied with artists, hung around with players in the fashion industry, and cut the hair of famous models. Not a bad life. It was actually kind of a wild life. It made sense that his son was a little wild, too.

Eventually Mr. Ohno made his way back to Seattle. There he opened his salon, Yuki's Diffusions. It was 1980 and he was putting down some roots. But while the traveling was slowing down, the fun was not.

Mr. Ohno continued to live a wild life, staying out late, partying with his friends, and occasionally flying off to London to cut a model's hair. Then he met Apolo's mother, Jerrie, and Mr. Ohno's life looked like it was finally going to settle down.

Unfortunately, a peaceful family life was not

in the cards. Apolo was born and Jerrie left. Mr. Ohno had gone from rebellious partier to family man to single dad, all in a few short years. Things definitely changed, but probably not the way Mr. Ohno had imagined they would.

But he didn't shy away from his responsibilities. He was thirty-seven, a hard worker, and he did everything he could for his son. He describes himself as half mom and half dad. Every Mother's Day Mr. Ohno would ask Apolo's teacher to convince Apolo to make him a card.

"I didn't want him to feel left out," Mr. Ohno says.

Apolo also got to hang out with other adults who took an interest in him. Whenever he'd get a break from school, he'd spend time at his dad's salon, sitting in the back and chatting with the customers. Mr. Ohno's regular clients still talk about their time with Apolo—especially these days, since almost everyone in Seattle is talking about the speed skating phenomenon.

Mr. Ohno and Apolo also found lots of ways to have fun together. Seattle is located near a beautiful coastline and spectacular mountains. The two spent lots of time in the wilderness of Washington State, hiking, camping, and swimming. One of their favorite spots was a place called Copalis Beach, nearly a hundred and fifty miles outside of Seattle. They used to rent a cabin there to retreat from the city. They'd walk for hours along the ocean and through the forests that lined the shore.

The situation worked well. It's not easy being a single dad, but Mr. Ohno and Apolo found a way to manage.

By the time Apolo was eight, he had started taking care of himself after school. He was a good student and was able to do his homework, make dinner, and put himself to bed without his father's help.

The main thing that still worried Mr. Ohno was Apolo's slightly wild streak—the same thing that had caused him to jump the fences at day care. To deal with all of Apolo's extra energy, Mr. Ohno encouraged him to pursue sports. Swimming and in-line skating were Apolo's favorites, and they were great physical outlets for him. And Apolo was good—better than most of the kids he swam and skated with. In fact, he got so good that he started competing. His dad drove him from competition to competition, even going as far as Canada for skate meets. Eventually Apolo took a state breast-stroke championship and a national in-line skating title in his age group.

But somehow these sports were never quite

enough for Apolo. He loved to compete and he loved speed. Still, in-line skating and swimming didn't quite do the trick. Then one day Apolo and his father turned on the TV. It was 1994, and they wanted to catch some of the Winter Olympics. That was when Apolo saw something that absolutely captivated him.

The Olympics that year were in Lillehammer, Norway, and a new sport was getting a lot of attention. It was called short track speed skating, and it had only been in the Olympics for two years. When Apolo and his father flipped on the TV, it was the first time either had seen the sport. They were totally mesmerized.

The speed, the shining skates, the slick ice, the body contact, the crashes, the spandex suits, the neon helmets—everything fascinated them. It was unlike anything they had ever seen. Apolo and his father were hooked. They couldn't turn it off. Apolo instantly knew that this was the sport for him.

Short track speed skating is a bit like traditional speed skating in that it's a bunch of people racing on ice skates. But it's also different from long track speed skating in a few important ways. First (as you might have guessed), it's on a shorter track. It's 111 meters long, to be exact. This means that there are more curves than on the longer track, and the curves are much tighter. When the skaters fly into a turn, they lean so far over that they touch the ice with their hands. By the time they straighten up, they have to start leaning into another curve.

Picture a motorcycle race. That's what short track looks like.

A second important feature of short track speed skating is that it's done in packs. Four or five people line up together, and the first person across the finish line wins. Long track skaters are timed. They don't race head-to-head with opponents.

Skating in packs adds a few things to short track speed skating. One is strategy. It's not enough to skate fast. You have to skate smart. You've got to dodge opponents, avoid collisions, and time your moves to hit the finish line first.

The other thing it adds is physical contact. In fact, a lot of people call it a contact sport. Short track skaters can reach speeds of thirty-five miles per hour, and when five people are scrambling at that speed together—all on blades only one millimeter wide—the results can be pretty spectacular. Crashes are common, and when someone wipes out, often the whole pack will go flying into the side rails. It sometimes looks a little like roller derby, except the racers are some of the best athletes in the world.

It's exciting stuff—just the thing for a kid with too much energy. That day in 1994 as he sat watching the Olympics with his dad, Apolo was totally blown away. He definitely wanted to do it.

The real question was how to talk his dad into letting him do something so obviously dangerous. Fortunately for Apolo, his father was already thinking the same thing. He was already thinking that this might be a good sport for Apolo.

"We both clicked, simultaneously," Mr. Ohno says. "The next Christmas, Santa brought a brand-new pair of skates."

CHAPTER TWO:

Early Success, Early Trouble

New skates. That was a start.

But getting into speed skating takes a lot of effort. Ice time can cost nearly a hundred and fifty dollars an hour. Coaching is expensive, and hard to find in Seattle. And unlike places like Minnesota and Wisconsin, Seattle doesn't have any frozen lakes that a young skater can work out on.

Still, Apolo's mind was made up, and Mr. Ohno was willing to help his son get into the sport. He enrolled Apolo in the Tacoma Speed Skating Club and started carting him around to practices and competitions.

All the driving was tough work. Mr. Ohno was a busy guy. But Apolo needed a way to blow off steam, and this seemed like a healthy way to do it.

How did Apolo do?

After just a little training, it was more than clear that getting into short track had been no mistake. This was Apolo's sport. Breakneck speeds, head-to-head competition, and the danger of crashing—it was just what Apolo was looking for.

There was something else Apolo liked about short track. He happened to be extremely good at it. The razor-sharp blades and the slick ice were new to Apolo. But he had put in a lot of time on in-line skates.

It wasn't long before he got the hang of short track and started proving himself in the Tacoma Speed Skating Club. And it wasn't long after that that he took his talents to the national level.

During his first year of skating, Apolo became a serious contender on the junior circuit. He went to places like Chicago and Canada to face off against other twelve-year-old skaters. More driving and flying for Mr. Ohno. More exhaustion and juggling work schedules. But it was worth it to him. He loved watching his son skate. So did the other people who came to the short track races.

Apolo was an immediate star. The crowds

were dazzled by this new kid from Seattle.

But Mr. Ohno could see that short track just might turn into something a little more than a pastime. Apolo was a natural. A prodigy. There was no explaining it, but he was just *better* than everyone else.

During that first year, Apolo even made it to the Junior World Championships in Milwaukee, Wisconsin, where he challenged the best young short track speed skaters in the world. It was here that Apolo proved that he wasn't just a kid with some talent; it looked like he could become one of the best in the sport. This became especially clear when he grabbed a world record in the twelve-year-olds' division of the 1,000-meter. Not bad for a kid who had only started speed skating less than a year earlier. Mr. Ohno was astounded.

So all this was good news. Apolo was off to a good start.

Unfortunately, not everything was going well in Apolo's life. On the rink, this kid was a dream. Off the rink, he was starting to face some problems.

To hear Apolo talk today, you'd think that he and his father have been best buds for Apolo's whole life. On camera and in newspaper interviews, he always says the same thing: "The relationship between my father and me is one of the best relationships you can have between a father and a son." He even says that his father is the biggest inspiration in his life. You don't hear that coming out of the mouths of too many teenagers.

But all the talk about how close he is with his father is what Apolo the nineteen-year-old Olympic champion says. Go back six or seven years to when he was just starting out on the short track and you get a very different story.

By the time Apolo was twelve, his wild streak was leading to major problems. His grades started plummeting, he was getting into trouble at school, and he was staying out late into the night without telling his father where he was or what he was doing. He basically started rebelling against everything he could find, beginning with his dad.

"I was rough," Apolo says. "If my dad said yes, I said no. That's the way it was for years."

A big part of Apolo's problem was the people he was spending time with.

"I had a lot of friends who were gangbangers," he says. "It wasn't healthy. I was hanging out with eighteen- and nineteen-year-olds, and they'd take me to a lot of house parties."

Worse, drinking, smoking, and vandalism were all part of the scene he was hanging out in. Apolo would disappear for days at a time, staying with his older friends, going to house parties, and not coming home. He started blowing off school and failing tests. It didn't take long for the former honor student to get kicked out of the honors program.

It was not really the behavior you'd expect from a future Olympic athlete.

Needless to say, Mr. Ohno was always in a state of panic. What father wouldn't be? He wanted Apolo to focus on school and skating and to get out of the bad group he was hanging around. But Apolo refused.

"And he didn't know how bad those guys really were," Apolo told a writer at *Sports Illustrated*. "One guy was in the newspaper every week for the houses and cars he robbed. People got shot, people got stabbed—or went to jail."

But it was hard for Mr. Ohno to know what to do. He tried to rein in Apolo. He tried to set limits, encourage him in school, keep him focused on sports. He even threatened military school.

But nothing seemed to work.

The one positive thing in Apolo's life was skating. It wasn't keeping him out of trouble, but it gave him something to focus on besides his crazy friends and staying out all night. And the short track promised a reward. It was clear to everyone that if Apolo played his cards right, he might have a serious future as a speed skater. The trouble was making sure he didn't waste his talent.

Following the Milwaukee Junior World Championships, Apolo continued to distinguish himself on the ice. He went to meets, won competitions, and practiced when he could. And even when he wasn't keeping up with his workout schedule, he was still doing well at tournaments.

His short but powerful frame was ideal for the short track. Apolo was a naturally gifted skater, and even when he was out of shape, he could do well in races.

But Apolo and Mr. Ohno started asking, What was next? Sure, Apolo was a natural. But at the highest levels of speed skating, being a natural isn't enough. You need top-flight training and conditioning. And you need to be absolutely dedicated to the ice.

Apolo loved skating, but he wasn't exactly dedicated to things like workouts or healthy diets.

A solution presented itself at a junior competition in Saratoga Springs, New York, where Mr. Ohno had taken Apolo to compete. After the competition started, a speed skating coach named Pat Wentland, from Lake Placid's Olympic Training Center, dropped by to check out the young talent.

He was impressed with what he saw. Short track speed skating was a relatively new sport. He was happy to see that so many kids were getting involved. But one skater stood out from all the rest. Apolo.

Wentland saw a lot of great skaters at the competition, but Apolo was a born champion. He could see it right away.

And it wasn't just because Apolo was already performing so well. What Wentland also saw at Saratoga Springs was potential. Some of the best skaters at Saratoga Springs were getting close to their natural limits. Apolo looked like he was just going to get better and better. He was a skating machine. With his short and stocky frame and his powerful legs, he was perfectly built for the short track. His muscular legs allowed him to burst off the line and charge forward at the end of a race. His short, broad build gave him a low center of gravity that let him easily take the fast curves of the track.

More important, Apolo had the mind of a short track racer. He had the rapid-fire brain that could lead him through tight packs of skaters at chilling speeds.

Before long, Wentland was talking to Apolo's father. He was discussing Apolo's future and what Apolo planned to do next. Mr. Ohno described his son's training, where they were from, and what Apolo's talents were. Eventually Wentland brought up the possibility of enrolling Apolo in the speed skating residency program at the Lake Placid Olympic Training Center.

There were some problems with this proposal. It would mean Apolo living away from home—nearly twenty-eight hundred miles. That's a lot to ask of a young teen. And the fact was that Mr. Ohno would miss his son. Apolo could really give his father a hard time, but Mr. Ohno would still miss him. Another problem was that Apolo hadn't demonstrated that he was all that responsible. Who knew what kind of trouble he could get into if his father weren't around? Mr. Ohno could guess the answer to this question. The answer was that Apolo could get into a *lot* of trouble.

And there was kind of a big problem. Apolo was only thirteen years old, and the rules of the training center said that athletes in residence had to be at least fifteen. And this wasn't just a formality. The Olympic Committee works hard not to put too much pressure on young athletes. Thirteen is a young age to be leaving home and dedicating yourself to a sport.

Apolo was special. There was no doubt about that. Wentland could see that this kid could end up as one of the best skaters on his squad—even at such a young age. Mr. Ohno knew this, too. He could see that Apolo was already surpassing the other teens he was skating against.

There was another incentive for Mr. Ohno. It was true that Apolo could get himself into trouble pretty easily. On the other hand, living in Seattle wasn't really helping. Mr. Ohno worked and couldn't always keep his eye on his son. Lake Placid's Olympic Training Center promised almost constant supervision.

And if Apolo did mess up, there was a natural limit to the trouble he could get into. There weren't any gangs roving around Lake Placid—no kids with guns, no crime, no big-city temptations that might distract a thirteen-year-old.

It seemed like a good option.

After talking about it for a while, Mr. Ohno and Coach Wentland decided that they should get Apolo admitted to the training center. But there were other people who had to approve the decision.

Wentland went to talk to his bosses and to the center's administrators. The minimum-age rule was pretty strictly enforced. If Apolo were allowed in, he'd be the youngest person ever to join the center. But Wentland made a passionate plea. With the center's help, he said, Apolo had the potential to be the best in the world. Age was irrelevant. This kid had talent and had earned the right to be there.

Eventually the training center officials approved Wentland's request. They agreed to admit Apolo. It was great news. Wentland had found a kid he could turn into a star, and Mr. Ohno had figured out a way to keep his son out of trouble.

There was only one problem: Apolo was completely against the idea.

And he wasn't going to make it easy on his father or his new coach.

CHAPTER
THREE:

A Skater Goes to Camp

June 1996. Apolo had just turned fourteen. He was in Seattle, getting ready to head to the Olympic Training Center at Lake Placid, where he'd join his new coach, Pat Wentland.

It was a great opportunity. All the same, Apolo wasn't happy.

He had friends in Seattle he didn't want to leave. He wasn't ready to work as hard as they'd make him in Lake Placid. And he was just generally a rebel. He didn't want to go just because his father thought it was a good idea. Still, what choice did he have? He packed his bags, grabbed his skates, said his good-byes, and he and his dad drove off to the airport.

Mr. Ohno was happy. He was fiercely proud of his son. Even when Apolo was in trouble, Mr.

Ohno knew he could make something of himself. And on the drive to the airport, Apolo seemed to be embarking on an exciting and important adventure.

Apolo was calm. He didn't want to go. But he wasn't frightened that morning. He wasn't sad. He wasn't scared of the training center. He wasn't even worried about the work. He was relaxed.

But this wasn't because he had accepted his fate. It was because he had hatched a plan to get out of it.

Apolo's father got him to the airport and let him out at the entrance. Father and son said good-bye. Apolo grabbed his bags and headed inside. Mr. Ohno drove off. Then, Apolo put his bags down and found a pay phone.

In the next instant he was on the phone to a friend, telling him to pick him up at the airport. He wasn't getting on the plane to Lake Placid. He wasn't going to the Olympic Training Center. He was staying in Seattle, and it didn't matter what his father or Coach Wentland wanted.

Reflecting on that time, Apolo says, "I made a call, and I was out. I had it all planned. Dad told me, 'I know what's best for you; you need to listen.' He comes from that Asian background; he's strict. But I'm fourteen—I don't want to do anything anybody says."

In a little while Apolo was in his friend's car and headed back to Seattle.

But Apolo wasn't entirely mean-spirited. He knew his dad would be worried, so he called and let Mr. Ohno know he was all right. The only thing Apolo didn't say was where he was.

Once the worry stopped, the anger came. Mr. Ohno was furious. Not only was this frustrating for him, but Apolo was giving up a great opportunity. Apolo loved short track speed skating, and he was a born competitor. Time in Lake Placid was the only way he'd ever make it into the elite ranks of speed skaters.

Wentland was a little upset himself. He had gone out on a limb for this kid, and he hadn't even showed up. If there had been any doubts about Apolo's maturity, they were now confirmed. Wentland was starting to wonder if this was going to be a big mistake.

Still, Apolo wasn't giving in. He kept his whereabouts a secret for a whole week. Finally Mr. Ohno called his ex-wife's sister, who lived in Portland, Oregon. She came up to Seattle to talk to her nephew. This was a drastic move, since

Mr. Ohno and Apolo were never in touch with his mother's family.

The next time Apolo called home to check in, Mr. Ohno passed the phone to Apolo's aunt. Apolo knew how worried his dad must be if his aunt had come up to Seattle. He had to give in. Apolo eventually told his aunt where he was and said he was coming home, finally putting an end to his escapade.

The next step was getting him onto the plane.

Mr. Ohno went to Lake Placid with Apolo this time. He knew that unless he escorted Apolo all the way to the Olympic Training Center, anything could happen. Mr. Ohno drove him to the airport, walked him through check-in, took him through security, and sat next to him on the plane. And once they made it to New York State, Mr. Ohno went all the way to the training center with his son. He wasn't taking any chances this time.

Finally, at the training center, Mr. Ohno was able to say good-bye to his son with some relief. He warned Wentland that he was going to have his hands full and wished him luck. Then he headed home.

It was tough, but Mr. Ohno knew he was

doing the right thing. In Seattle, Apolo only faced more trouble. At the training center, he'd be in a controlled environment. Best of all, he'd learn to skate like a champion.

Still, there were other challenges ahead. They had gotten Apolo to the training center.

But that didn't mean that they could make him work.

Apolo went along with the activities, but only half-heartedly. He missed his friends. He missed Seattle. And he hated Lake Placid. He was physically present at the training center, but mentally and emotionally, he was miles away.

"I was so young," he says, talking about those days, "totally rebellious against anything my dad or anybody in authority said. I hated the first month I was in Lake Placid. Moving from Seattle to New York is such a big change. Especially Lake Placid. It's just such a small town. I had never been in that kind of environment. I just felt kind of caged."

But even though it was a small town, there were still plenty of opportunities for Apolo to goof off. For one thing, he just refused to work hard. He'd put in his time but never gave anything extra—and giving extra is essential for top-level athletes. If there was an easy way out, he'd take it.

He was also more deliberate about his slacking. One of Apolo's favorite tricks came on the five-mile runs from the training center to the lake. The whole squad would run to the lake together, but Apolo would take a little detour. He'd stop off at the local Pizza Hut and gorge himself on pizza. When the pack was on its way back, he'd join up with them again and slowly run back to camp.

For a potential Olympic athlete, this kind of behavior was insane. Not only was he blowing off his workout, he was also eating pizza—a killer food for people competing at top levels. The heavy fats and empty calories only hurt Apolo's performance. In fact, Apolo was so much fatter than the rest of the skaters that they called him "Chunky."

That's a pretty unflattering nickname for a top-notch athlete.

So what turned Apolo around? Probably a lot of things. Being called "Chunky" was one of them. Every day Apolo was surrounded by athletes in peak physical condition, and being known as slow and chubby was not the reputation he wanted for himself. But most important was Apolo's athletic spirit and competitive nature. In other words, Apolo was used to winning, but his slacking off had made him the worst skater in camp.

Coach Wentland describes a specific day when he thinks things really changed. The coaches were testing the body fat of the skaters. When they tested Apolo, all the trips to Pizza Hut finally caught up with him. He had the highest body fat of anybody. In fact, his body fat was almost double that of most of the other skaters. The numbers were there for everyone to see.

It was completely humiliating.

After that, things were different for Apolo. He had been at the training center for about a month. The shock of the new surroundings was starting to wear off. He missed his friends less. But most of all, he didn't want to be at the bottom of the pack anymore. He knew he was better than that. He might even be the best short track skater in camp. But his potential was irrelevant if he didn't live up to it. It was time for Apolo to get to work.

He approached Coach Wentland to tell him he was ready to take things more seriously. In fact, he told Wentland that he was there to be the best speed skater in the camp. He didn't want to be the fattest and the slowest. He wanted to be on top, and he was willing to work for it.

Still, he was just a fourteen-year-old kid with only a month of training at the Olympic Center under his belt. He was good. But there were lots of people who were good.

Were Apolo's words the voice of a determined athlete, or was this just an overconfident kid who thought he was better than everyone else?

CHAPTER
FOUR:

A New Commitment

Things changed in the summer of 1996. Once Apolo committed himself, he started proving that he had the talent that Wentland first noticed when he first saw him race in Saratoga Springs.

But doing well at the camp was just the first step. There was something else on Apolo's mind, and as he continued training it became an obsession. It was the thing that had clicked with him two years earlier when he first learned about the sport.

There was a big prize on the horizon. It wasn't beating his campmates. It wasn't even grabbing world records. It was the Olympics, and it wasn't even just the Olympics.

It was winning gold at the Olympics.

The next Olympics were in Nagano, Japan, in 1998. They were a year and a half off. When the Nagano games started, Apolo would be just fifteen. Most speed skaters hit their prime skating years in their twenties. For a fourteen-year-old to think he could be the best in the world was completely outrageous. But outrageous dreams are what make great Olympic champions.

So, Pizza Hut was out. Apolo started completing the five-mile runs and demanding more of himself. He woke up at 6 A.M. without complaining. He focused on what his coaches told him. He worked out as hard as he could. He built up his muscles, refined his skating technique, and developed an almost supernatural sense for the strategy of the short track.

Taking a corner at thirty-five miles an hour is one thing. But you've got to be able to do it with three guys next to you. That's the skill that separates short track from the time-based long track. And it's this almost unteachable skill that sets the winners apart from the losers. In a 1,000-meter race, you don't necessarily want to be in the lead the whole time. You want to hold your place and then suddenly burst ahead. What counts is who makes it across the finish line first. That takes a sense of timing, a sense of when to make your move. Apolo had that sense. He understood the mental elements better than anyone. And more and more, he started making it across the finish line first.

But there was more than just the training camp. Soon Apolo was venturing out of Lake Placid and hitting the competition circuit. He was still competing at the junior level. It was good experience. But he also raced in the overall events, against the best skaters of all ages. He was as good as anyone out there. And to the amazement of Coach Wentland, Apolo's teammates, Apolo's opponents, and Mr. Ohno, he just kept getting better and better. In fact, in 1997, when he was still just fourteen, he proved that he was not only a contender. He proved he was one of the best in the world.

It was at the U.S. National Short Track Championships—a great predictor of who would make the Olympic team. He'd still have to do well at the Olympic trials to go to Nagano. But if he put in a good performance at the National Championships first, his chances would be very good indeed.

And perform well he did, although "well" is an understatement. Apolo's performance at the National Championships was nothing short of remarkable. The trouble-making kid from Seattle who'd hidden at the Pizza Hut in Lake Placid rather than run with his team proceeded to win race after race. Almost every time he stepped on the ice, he crossed the finish line first.

The competition was shocked. Wentland and the other skaters knew Apolo was good, but no one had expected the kind of performance he put in. Clearly Apolo had straightened himself out. The overnight prankster with the sullen attitude was nowhere to be seen at the National Champioships.

When it was all over, Apolo had won the National Overall Short Track Speed Skating title, beating out contenders who were almost twice his age.

Everyone was completely floored. Apolo had arrived. He had proved to himself and everyone else that his place at the Lake Placid Olympic Training Center was deserved. His performance was no fluke. He was the best in the country.

And he was just fourteen!

But being the best in the country still fell short of Apolo's goals. He was looking to be the best in the world. It was gold in Nagano that Apolo was after. That would be the ultimate competition. But Apolo would have to prove himself in a different arena if he wanted the chance to compete there.

First he had to do well at the Olympic trials if he was even going to make it to Nagano.

CHAPTER
FIVE:

The Turning Point

By the time Apolo turned fifteen, there was little doubt of what he was capable of. He was winning national races and doing well in world competitions. He was keeping a cool head, racing smart, and growing in strength and endurance.

But just as before, raw talent wasn't always enough. Apolo was now dividing his time between Lake Placid, competitions around the world, and Seattle. And when he was back in Seattle, he slipped back into the same life he was living before he went to the Olympic Training Center in upstate New York.

He'd get home, and before long, he'd be back with his friends. He'd disobey his dad. He'd spend nights away from the house. And his scene was just the same as it had always been—the gangs, the drinking, the smoking had not disappeared while he was in Lake Placid.

Staying focused and committed to a sport is hard enough. With the kind of distractions Apolo found in Seattle, it was a million times worse. And he was still just a teenager—most kids his age were worrying about things like math quizzes and prom dates, not how to avoid bullets and be a world-class athlete.

And there were other pressures. The fact was that Apolo was the best short track skater in the country. There were a lot of people who thought he could win gold in Nagano. He wasn't just trying to achieve a personal goal. His victories and his defeats would be felt by everyone in the country. Bring back a gold from Japan and the nation rejoices. Fail and you've failed your country.

And there was one more issue. Apolo's father was from Japan, and that was where most of Apolo's family lived. His aunts, uncles, cousins, and grandparents would all be there to cheer him on. They'd all be bragging to their friends about their world-famous Olympic relative. The possibility of racing in front of his family was thrilling. It was also terrifying.

Between the medals, the grandparents, and the coaches, the pressure was intense.

Too intense.

The Olympic trials were held in Lake Placid, New York, and when Apolo made his return from Seattle with his father at his side, he was exhausted, unfocused, overweight, and out of shape. It was almost as though the past year's work had been for naught.

Just as at the Nationals, he lined up on the ice again and again. But this time things were different. He was slow off the line, he rarely took the lead, and he never had the energy to put in a strong finish. Most important, his mental edge was gone. He wasn't skating smart, and it was killing him. In race after race, he was the last to cross the finish line.

There were sixteen people at Lake Placid trying to make the Olympic squad. When it was all over, Apolo had placed dead last. Sixteenth out of sixteen. He was devastated. His earlier performances now meant nothing. He was not going to the 1998 Winter Olympics.

When Apolo boarded the plane back to Seattle, his career suddenly seemed like a wreck. In a few short years, Apolo had lived through what most people never even experience in a lifetime: early promise, stunning success, and bitter failure. It was a lot for a teenager to be thinking about, and what lay ahead seemed even more confusing.

Apolo wasn't the only one with doubts. Coach Wentland was well aware of what Apolo was capable of. But he also knew how important focus and desire were to the short track. Apolo had lost that focus and that desire, and those qualities might prove hard to regain.

Apolo's father was also uncertain. But he was not disappointed for himself. He was mostly concerned for his son. Apolo had become a great skater not because of Mr. Ohno or Coach Wentland. Apolo had become great because it was what he himself had wanted.

Mr. Ohno wanted to make sure that Apolo wasn't going to lose something that he had worked so hard for. It was Apolo's dream to go to the Olympics, and Mr. Ohno didn't want his son to have any regrets in his life.

When they got back to Seattle, Mr. Ohno arranged for Apolo to take a trip. It was up to Apolo which way his skating career would go, but Mr. Ohno wanted to make sure that his son had the time and freedom to think the problem over. He rented a cabin on a deserted shore of Washington State, drove his son there, and left him on his own for a week. He had food, water, and his cat. But that was it. There was no television, no telephone, no friends dropping by to hang out.

It would be a chance for Apolo to clear his head, to think things through. If Apolo were going to be a short track champion, he'd have to come to the decision on his own.

His father could live with either decision one way or another. He wanted to make sure his son could live with it as well.

At first the whole thing was pretty confusing. Apolo was exhausted and defeated. Speed skating promised so much fun and so much glory, but it had also led to the biggest disappointment of his life. If he returned, it was going to be hard work. And there were no guarantees. He could devote himself to the short track for the next four years and still blow it at the Olympic trials.

On the other side of the coin, Apolo couldn't quite imagine another future for himself. There was no job, no career waiting for him. He had finally started to realize just where his Seattle friends would lead him—nowhere. He didn't really want to return to that crowd.

Still, you can't struggle to get to the Olympics just because you can't think of anything else to do.

During his week alone, he thought about it over and over. But answers didn't seem to be coming. There was only confusion. The question seemed to become more and more puzzling.

Then one day Apolo went out for a run, hoping to clear his mind with some exercise. He ran along a road by the shore, thinking about where his life had led him. After a while, it started to rain, and a hole in his shoe started to cause a blister on his foot. As he kept running, the rain got harder and his foot hurt more and more.

He soon exhausted himself and sat down, weary and confused, on a rock by the side of the road. His foot throbbed. The rain stung his face. He was cold and wet.

The whole situation was like his life. He was stuck in the middle of nowhere, nothing seemed to be going his way, and he wasn't sure if he had the strength to carry on.

But as he considered recent events, blocking out the pelting rain and his stinging foot, things began to crystallize in his mind. The connection between his position on that rock and the crossroads in his life became more and more clear. He was tired, defeated, demoralized. But he still had options. He had two, to be exact.

He could sit there feeling sorry for himself, or he could get up and continue on. The decision of what to do about the small problem on the roadside quickly became the larger decision he was making about his life. And the decision was all his.

Would he be angry, disappointed, frustrated?

Would he give up, hang his head, and walk away from speed skating?

Or would he have the strength to get up and try again?

Would he be able to accept his defeat at the Olympic trials, dust himself off, and get back on the short track?

Finally he reached a conclusion.

Apolo stood up and kept running. He didn't turn back. He didn't slow down. He ran faster and faster, putting the beating rain and the growing blister out of his mind.

It was at that moment that Apolo decided to return to the short track.

Looking back on that episode in his life, Apolo knows that the week at the cabin was probably the most important turning point in his career. As he said later on, "During that week, it just came to me that this was something I was meant to do. I was given a gift to skate, and this [was] something I wanted to do. I came back so much stronger, hungrier, with more desire."

It was more than a decision to give skating another shot. It was a decision to be the best in the world and not let anything stand in his way. Whether it happened or not was still a question. But his decisions about what to work for, what he wanted, what his goals were, were final: he was returning to the short track, and he was going to be the best in the world.

CHAPTER
SIX:

The Journey to Salt Lake

No doubt about it, not making the Olympics was devastating for Apolo. It's hard to put a good spin on that kind of disappointment.

However, Apolo's defeat in Lake Placid gave him the will to compete even harder. His sights were set on the 2002 Winter Olympics in Salt Lake City, Utah. He'd have the home court advantage, four more years of experience to draw from, and a brand-new chance to take home some medals.

He just had to make sure he did what it would take in the next bunch of years to make it there.

Oh, and he also wanted to have some fun along the way.

The next few years brought Apolo the kind

of success young athletes only dream about. He had to sit out the Olympics, but after the Nagano Games ended, he hit the short track skating circuit. He ceased to be just a national power and soon became the dominant force in world competition.

The racing circuit for short track is pretty confusing. There are lots of different competitions and lots of different categories and levels.

Basically, because of Apolo's age, he could compete on the junior level and on the regular, senior level. He entered every competition he could and started taking home titles in both divisions.

Obviously, the adult, or regular, short track category is a bit more important. That's the category where all the world's best can compete, no matter what their age. In this category, Apolo competed on both the national and world levels. And on both levels he excelled.

Right after the Nagano Games, he started establishing his importance at home. He won the national title again, proving he was still the best in the U.S. He was fifteen, and the skating world was again shocked by how young and how good this kid from Seattle was. He would win this title two more times in the years before the 2002 Olympics, and he never stopped amazing his competitors and the fans.

He also started showing his talent in the world arena, winning medal after medal in international events. To make things easy on competitors and fans, there is a system called the World Cup, monitored by the International Skating Union, that keeps track of who is winning the most. The World Cup system allots points based on how well a skater places in various races. The World Cup points are then added up to determine an overall ranking.

After the disappointment at the Olympic trials, Apolo started racking up World Cup points at a dizzying speed, moving in and out of the lead over the next few years. By 2001, however, he had established himself the undisputed champion. He was first in all three events (500-meter, 1,000-meter, and 1,500-meter) and was the overall World Cup champion. He had won an absolutely astounding fifteen World Cup gold medals that year! It was incredible that someone so young could hold all these titles. He was the best in the world, and the World Cup championships proved it.

Still, for all that success, there was one thing that weighed heavily on Apolo's mind: Salt Lake City and the 2002 Winter Olympics.

For almost all athletes, the Olympic Games have a strange kind of power. Despite the excitement of something like a World Cup speed skating competition, it's not the same. You can win all the World Cups you want, but without Olympic gold, you can never quite call yourself the very best. All of Apolo's victories had been great. But they were all part of his training for Salt Lake City.

The World Cup championships and the national titles brought him closer to Salt Lake. But the bigger hurdle lay in Kearns, Utah, at the end of 2001. This is where the Olympic trials were held. None of Apolo's victories would mean anything if he failed there.

And Apolo had a bad history with this event. Going into the trials for Nagano, Apolo was also considered the favorite, and he had blown it. Would Kearns be a repeat of that?

There are five events in the Olympic short

track trials: two time trials and three head-to-head race series (in the 500-meter, 1,000-meter, and 1,500-meter events). Each race carries a certain amount of points. The points also count toward who makes the team.

To make the team, a skater has to finish in the top six. Of that top six, only the top two get to compete in the individual races. Four are chosen for the relay. There are two alternates.

Given Apolo's performance in 2001, he was definitely the favorite in every race. But he had proven in the past that being the favorite means very little—you can still lose. On top of that, for a skater like Apolo, being the alternate or just a member of the relay team would be a big disappointment. For Apolo to feel happy, he'd have to take one of the top spots so he could compete in the individual races.

That meant winning a lot of races and scoring a lot of points.

And there was one other problem: luck. One of the great aspects of short track speed skating is the head-to-head competition. People can skate smart and pull off an upset. Or a favorite can take a corner too close to a competitor and wipe out, ending his chances with a single wrong move. There were lots of things that could go wrong. There was a lot for Apolo to think about, and he was always the first to say that talent wasn't everything. There were a lot of traps he'd have to avoid to win.

But these trials would stand in stark contrast to the 1998 trials. This time, Apolo was absolutely flawless.

He won every race and even set a world record. And he was having a blast.

This was not the overweight, tired partier who'd showed up in Lake Placid four years ago. Apolo was a well-oiled machine, and he was skating with the heart of a champion. Every race was like that rainy day at the cabin when he got up from the rock to keep running. Apolo knew what he wanted and what he had to do. And his performance was perfect.

But there is a lot of strategy involved in the short track Olympic trials. The competition happens just months before the actual Olympics, and while the skaters want to win, they also don't want to overdo it. Injuries can end hopes for a medal, and there are lots of injuries in short track. The sharp blades, blistering speeds, and spectacular crashes can ruin a career.

After Apolo had won the first seven races, he was guaranteed starting positions in each of the events. He was thousands of points ahead of the other competitors. So on the last night, December 22, when he came in third in the last race, it wasn't a shock. He was clearly better than all the other skaters. All the same, there were good reasons for Apolo not to skate his hardest. He had to maintain his health and stamina for the big show in February.

There was just one problem.

Apolo's third-place finish helped two of his friends, Rusty Smith and Shani Davis, make the team. It also meant that another opponent, Tom O'Hare, who was competing for the sixth spot, was off the team. And it meant that a competitor named Ron Biondo wouldn't qualify for the individual events.

Apolo's third-place finish had big consequences.

There was a lot of grumbling. And the grumbling intensified. And then, disaster followed.

A few weeks after the trials, Tom O'Hare filed formal charges against Apolo for fixing the race. That is, Tom was claiming that Apolo cheated. He said that Apolo did not go easy to avoid injury. He claimed instead that Apolo took third place to ensure that his friends made the team—at Tom and Ron's expense.

These were heavy accusations. If the Olympic Committee ruled that Apolo had thrown the race, it would be a major scandal. Apolo could easily be kicked off the team. The past four years, the hard work, the dedication—all would be down the drain.

And even if they didn't kick him off, the Olympics would still be tainted for Apolo. If he were branded a cheater, gold medals at the Olympics wouldn't be quite so sweet.

It looked like the Nagano speed skating trials all over again.

In mid-January, the case against Apolo went to arbitration. That meant that an independent judge was hired by the Olympic Committee to listen to the complaints.

The arbitrator in this case was a guy named James Holbrook. He had experience with this kind of thing. The Olympic Committee hoped he'd get to the bottom of the mystery as quickly and as smoothly as possible. Hearings were scheduled to last three days.

The hearings took place at the Olympic Training Center in Colorado Springs, Colorado. This

**That's my son!
Yuki Ohno films
Apolo during the
Olympic trials in
December 2001.**

[Above, left] Taking the lead in
the 1500m Olympic trials, where
Apolo would go on to set a world
short track speedskating record!
He clocked in at 2 minutes,
13.728 seconds.

[Below, left] Apolo strides ahead
of Italian speedskater Fabio Carta
during the men's 5000m relay
Olympic semifinals.

[This page] Apolo warms up for
the short track competition at the
Salt Lake Ice Center.

[This page, above] Apolo skates for the gold in the second heat of the Olympics 1500m short track.

[This page, below] Ouch! Apolo, along with Mathieu Turcotte of Canada and Ahn Hyun-Soo of Korea, struggles to get up off the ice after an accident during the 1000m short track.

[Next page, left] Dream come true! Apolo learns that he's won the gold in the men's 1500m short track.

[Next page, right] Apolo waves to the crowd after winning the 1500m Olympic qualifying race in October 2001.

[This page, above] A smiling Apolo responds to questions during a press conference for the US short track speedskating team.

[This page, below] Apolo flies across the ice during the second heat of the 500m short race.

[Next page, above] Apolo checks out the scoreboard after being disqualified for pushing during the men's semifinal 500m short track race.

[Next page, below left] Apolo chats with a teammate during practice.

[Next page, below right] After the collision during the 1000m finals, Apolo leaves the postrace press conference in a wheelchair.

[Above] Apolo skates right on the heels of Kim Dong-Sung of South Korea during the men's 1500m short track Olympic finals.

[Below] My first medal: Apolo displays his silver medal after being slowed by a collision in the 1000m Olympic finals. Steven Bradbury of Australia took the gold, and Matthieu Turcotte of Canada took the bronze.

had actually become Apolo's new home. It was where the top Olympic speed skaters trained along with many of the other elite winter athletes in the U.S.

The hearings put everyone at the center in a pretty bad mood. People at the training center were supposed to be happy, excited, and focused. The Olympics in Salt Lake were now only weeks away.

The hearings cast a shadow over the center and the entire winter team. No one wanted to accept the idea that Apolo might have thrown a race.

Most of the people involved with the case were present for the hearings. Some were there to testify. Others were there to support their friends.

The worst part of the case against Apolo was the witnesses who claimed they overheard Apolo talking to teammates Shani and Rusty about a plan to fix the race. These witnesses legally swore that Apolo had said that he was going to drop back to help them out. On top of that, the head referee, Jim Chapin, was saying that he thought Apolo purposely fell back to help out Shani. These were not good signs.

As people started to understand the case, another part of the scandal became clear. Ron Biondo, who finished fourth in the race, said that Apolo had been illegally blocking him. Had Ron beaten Rusty, Ron would have claimed one of the two individual spots on the team. Ron claimed that Apolo had been trying to help Rusty and that he had prevented Ron from beating him. Ron did not file formal charges. But his story backed up Tom O'Hare's story. And it didn't make Apolo look very good.

So what was the truth?

Well, countering the witnesses who said that Apolo had thrown the race, a bunch of other witnesses said the opposite. They claimed that Apolo didn't do anything unusual. Coaches also supported Apolo's claim that he took it easy to avoid injury. This was a smart way to race. Apolo didn't need to win. The most important thing was for him to stay healthy. On top of that, three other referees claimed that the race was clean.

It was a confusing problem. The arbitrator, James Holbrook, had his work cut out for him.

After three days of hearings, Holbrook finally came to a conclusion.

He had reviewed the evidence and decided that the case against Apolo was extremely weak. He thought that the witnesses' claims against Apolo were not adding up. And there were reports that the witnesses themselves had admitted their testimonies were false. Tom O'Hare realized he was not going to win his case and dropped it.

It was over. Apolo's name was cleared.

But the trial had still caused plenty of problems. The three days of hearings were three days that Apolo was not training. He had to be in top physical shape for Salt Lake. Just a few days' disruption from his training schedule could mean serious consequences.

More important were the mental costs. The trials were distracting. This was a time when Apolo should have been getting psyched for Salt Lake. Instead he spent a lot of time wondering if he was going to wash out like he did before Nagano.

Apolo knew he was innocent. All the same, that doesn't mean worst-case scenarios were not on his mind.

And there was the damage to the team. Not only did it throw off practice schedules, it caused a split in the relay squad. Ron Biondo would be racing with Apolo, and he had just testified against him. And when Holbrook found that Apolo hadn't done anything wrong, Biondo was clearly upset.

All the same, these were Olympic athletes. They were trained to rise above this kind of thing. And that's exactly what they did.

Rusty Smith and Ron Biondo had a heart-to-heart at a competition in Canada. They had different opinions, but they both wanted to win gold in the relay. They didn't agree on the ruling, but they agreed to work together. It was clear to both that the members of the relay team would not walk away best friends. But they decided that they *could* walk away with a medal.

The six-member squad also held a press conference to show the world they were united as a team. It was important for them to put the scandal behind them for their own sakes. It had already caused enough distraction. But it was also important to show a united front for the sake of the entire American team and for the Olympics itself. They wanted to put the matter to rest. And when they appeared before the press together, that's exactly what they did. Biondo said he was over it. Smith said he was, too. Apolo shrugged his shoulders in a good-natured way and said he just wanted to get back to the track. They were ready to move on.

The next stop was Salt Lake City. It was the real deal now. It was what they had all worked the last four years for. They didn't want anything else to spoil it.

Chapter Seven:

Staggering to Silver

Everyone who is in the Olympics has proven him- or herself to be a top-notch competitor. Apolo had done more than that. He had spent the last four years dominating the short track. In the year leading up to the Olympics, he seemed to win every time he stepped onto the ice.

So he was used to winning. And he was used to being the center of attention.

Still, all the training and all the experience couldn't quite prepare Apolo for the frenzy and excitement of the Olympics.

It was a unique event. It was what Apolo dreamed about when he went to bed at night. It was what he thought about at 6 A.M. when he was hitting the weights. And when opening day arrived and he walked past the crowds in the Rice-Eccles Olympic Stadium, he could barely catch his breath.

Even at a World Cup event, crowds are usually small. Short track is not a sport with a huge international audience like basketball or soccer. But this was the Olympics. Everyone was watching. And when he was with the rest of the American team—the bobsledders, the hockey players, the snowboarders—he knew that he was part of an elite group of people that millions of Americans were counting on.

And even in this elite group, Apolo was receiving special attention. First, people were speculating that he might be able to win four gold medals. It was a long shot, but Apolo was the best in the world in each of the short track events. Some people were even calling it "Apolo's Olympics" because he was such a favorite.

Apolo shrugged the predictions off. Four gold medals are almost impossible in short track speed skating, not because there's no clear favorite, but because so many unexpected things happen in short track. People crash, bump, and fall all the time. One misstep will take you out of the competition. It would be almost impossible for anyone to win four golds.

Still, people were hopeful. And as the Olympics were hyped on TV and in newspapers, the media grabbed hold of Apolo. He was interviewed on television, for newspapers, on the radio, and on the Internet. NBC, which was airing the games, was using Apolo to draw audiences. They put him on countless commercials, trying to get people to tune in.

Apolo was young, hip, and had a great smile. People were saying that Apolo looked less like an athlete and more like a rock star. His long wavy hair, his trademark bandana, the little beard he sported on his chin, and the diamond earring in his ear all made his the face of a new generation of Olympic contenders. Apolo could draw huge audiences of young people.

Probably the biggest hype Apolo got came from *Sports Illustrated*. Not only did they write a feature article about him, but they put him on the cover. Only the Michael Jordans and the Tiger Woodses of the world appear on the cover of *Sports Illustrated*. It was a huge honor. It was also pretty intimidating. People had high hopes for this nineteen-year-old. *Sports*

Illustrated was one of many magazines that were saying that Apolo could grab four gold medals.

Another reason Apolo was the center of so much attention was his background. He is Japanese American, and few minorities had ever competed on the U.S. Winter Olympic Team. The 2002 team had more minorities than any previous team. There were ten people from minority backgrounds out of the 211-member squad. That's still not many, but it represented an improvement over previous years.

Many people were hoping that these Olympics would bring even more minorities into winter sports. And if Apolo won gold, there was no telling how many young Asian Americans would be inspired to put on speed skates and start racing.

There was also Apolo's father. In some ways, his dad put the least pressure on him. The two had been getting along great in the time leading up to the Olympics. Apolo was older, more mature, less rebellious, and he didn't really have time for his old scene in Seattle. He wasn't rebelling against his dad anymore. His dad was his biggest fan.

Mr. Ohno could live with Apolo not winning. All the same, he had put in lots and lots of time guiding Apolo through his early days in the sport. Apolo wanted to do well for him. Mr. Ohno was going to be at every race and every practice. They were in it together, and Apolo didn't want to let him down.

And if Apolo won medals, there would be even bigger money for his future training expenses. The Olympic Committee had started a bonus system awarding athletes extra training money for every medal they brought home. Apolo, like the other athletes, would get $25,000 for every gold medal, $15,000 for every silver, and $10,000 for every bronze.

That training money was a big deal. It meant not having to borrow money to pay for coaching.

It meant not having to worry about getting ice time.

It meant not having to live on peanut butter and canned soup.

So there was lots and lots of pressure coming from all sides. Everywhere Apolo looked there was someone hoping he did well. Fortunately, by the time the teenager arrived in Salt Lake, he had been through a lot. The gangs, the trouble in school, the World Cup medals, the disappointment at the Nagano trials—all these things added up. They meant Apolo could take all the attention in stride and not get too bothered. In the end, there was really only one thing he had to think about: getting across the finish line of his races before his opponents did.

In some ways, it was really that simple.

Apolo had a few days to think about his strategy after the opening ceremonies. Opening day was on Friday, February 8, 2002. Apolo's first race was scheduled for day six of the Olympics—Wednesday, February 13. It was the opening heat for the 1,000-meter event. If he made it through the heats, the final would be that Saturday night—day nine.

So after the fanfare of the opening ceremonies, it was back to the rink. Apolo still had time to get some training in. He wanted to squeeze out every bit of practice he could before he launched his Olympic career.

Apolo was trying to stay focused. He was staying at the Olympic Village with the rest of the athletes. Most people there were pretty focused. But the Village can also be a fun place to hang out. There were lots of new people from faraway countries. There was lots to see and do. You could spend a week there staying up late talking to new friends and never getting the rest you needed.

But Apolo had dealt with distractions before. He knew how to stay on target. He was thinking about Wednesday night. His first race. The 1,000-meter race.

The mood around the Olympic Village was actually more relaxed than usual. A flu bug was going around, and people were getting sick. It was a nightmare for some. Athletes had spent their lives training for the two-week-long Olympics, and suddenly they were sick.

Unfortunately, one of the victims was Apolo.

He was philosophical about it. Unexpected things always crop up at competitions. He said he was ready and that the flu wouldn't prevent him from winning.

Still, it was not the way he'd wanted to start out.

He put his sickness out of his mind and practiced. He rehearsed the 1,000-meter over and over in his head. He thought about his opponents, all of whom he had raced before. He thought about their abilities, their strategies, and how he could match them. Finally, Wednesday came. His first race. He was ready. Or so he thought.

Apolo later described the whole thing as breathtaking. He trained and prepared as much as possible, but when he stepped onto the ice, he was blown away.

The race was held at the Delta Center, home to the NBA's Utah Jazz. It was an arena built for huge spectacles, and Apolo's appearance was every bit as spectacular as any NBA championship game.

By the time he skated onto the ice, everyone in the crowd knew his story. They knew about the troubled kid who'd beat the odds and made it to the Olympics. They knew about the teen phenom who had swept the 2001 World Cup. They knew about the trouble he had given his father and how close the two were now. Mr. Ohno was almost as much of a spectacle as Apolo—people stared at him and the television cameras were trained on him, all watching the proud father keep an eye on his boy.

Everything seemed to be focused on Apolo's story. Everyone seemed to be there to watch the kid they had been hearing so much about. And they were there to cheer him on.

His first reception was probably one of the wildest of the whole Olympics. The arena was packed to capacity. There were over 15,000 people there, every one of them screaming at the top of their lungs. "U-S-A, U-S-A," they chanted.

People held up signs saying things like OHNO, OH YES! and MISSION APOLO. The announcer could barely be heard over the noise of the fans. The whole scene seemed to reflect the freshness of the new young sport of short track. Traditional winter sports can have a stuffy quality. Short track events were like aerial skiing or the snowboarding halfpipe—they had more the spirit of a skate park than a formal international competition.

And the fans were definitely hip to the scene. People sported tattoos, dyed hair, and ear-rings—not that far from Apolo's look. And it wasn't just the fans. The Olympic officials had gone along with the skate-park spirit. Music from rock bands like Creed and Van Halen was blasting over the loud speakers. But again, all the music and all the mayhem seemed to have purpose—people were there to see Apolo, and they were there to see him win.

Apolo could hardly believe what he saw. He

had skated in a lot of competitions, but nothing had prepared him for this.

"I can't even describe how I felt," he later told the press. "My heart rate was definitely pumped up. I worked hard just to stay relaxed."

He went to the Delta Center trying to think of how to make it to the finish line. When he got there, he had to deal with being a star.

Still, as usual, he took the new experience well. He focused on his task: doing well in his races so he could qualify for the finals. And once the gun went off and Apolo started swooping around the ice, the crowd disappeared. There were only his opponents and the finish line.

Here was where Apolo, the master skater, began to shine. Nothing was distracting him— no flu, no chanting, no memories of the Nagano trials. In his qualifying races that Wednesday night, there was only him and the ice, and he performed just as everyone had hoped. He was sensational.

But you have to win a lot of races to win a medal. Wednesday night was a good start, but it was only a start. The biggest test of his life would come on Saturday night.

His first final. The 1,000-meter. This race was not a qualifier. If you did well, you walked away with a medal. If you lost, it was all over.

Saturday night at the Delta Center was like Wednesday night in many ways. But the stakes were higher, and the crowd was even more frenzied. This time the fans were not only going to be treated to a great night of races—they were also going to see skaters on the podium, bowing their heads and accepting medals. The coaches were there to see their pupils do what they had been training them to do for years. Mr. Ohno was nervously watching the rink, hoping his son achieved everything he wanted to. Despite the anxiety, there was also a sense of calm. All bets were on Apolo for the gold. He was the best out there. Everyone knew that the race was his.

There were five racers in the 1,000-meter final: Apolo, Li Jiajun from China, Ahn Hyun Soo from South Korea, Mathieu Turcotte from Canada, and Steven Bradbury from Australia. These were the five best 1,000-meter short track racers in the world. Apolo knew them all. He had raced against them all. He knew that he could beat them.

But he also knew that under the right circumstances, they could beat him. In the rough and wild sport of short track speed skating, there was no telling what would happen.

As they lined up, it was like the races on the previous Wednesday night. One moment Apolo was hearing his name chanted and seeing the flags waving. The next moment it was just him and the ice, waiting for the gun to go off. He had to concentrate. He possessed the physical ability. There was no question about that. But the pressure of the finals and the big stakes waiting at the end of the race made this a mental game. He had to focus.

When the gun went off, Apolo was off the line quickly. He had to get a good start, and he did. The pack was tight, but he quickly grabbed the lead.

The 111-meter track was glistening beneath the five racers as they bent into the tight turns. The skate blades are only one millimeter thick. There's not much room for mistakes. A slight wobble, a bump in the ice, a misplaced hand can mean the end for the racers. But they were smooth and controlled. This was the Olympics and they were the world's best 1,000-meter racers. They all knew what they were doing.

As they whipped around the turns, they leaned in, coming around at such steep angles that they touched the ice with their hands before straightening up again. Around and around they went. It was a nine-lap race. They had to play it smart. They couldn't move too early or too late. But by the seventh lap, the racers were skating hard for position.

Apolo was clearly in the lead. He was the man to beat. He knew it. The fans knew it. And the other opponents knew it. They tried to get around him but couldn't. Apolo was just too fast. Turn after turn he held the lead.

Lap eight ended. Lap nine began. He was still ahead. But he had to hold on. His opponents were breathing down his neck.

As they approached the final turn, Apolo still held the lead. But now the finish line was in sight. Apolo had been here before and he knew what it would take to get across first. Victory was in his sights.

But Apolo was still being challenged. Li Jiajun of China was coming around on Apolo's outside, and Ahn Hyun Soo of South Korea was right behind him. They were moving at thirty-five miles per hour and were only inches away from each other.

Suddenly, twenty meters from the finish line, Li Jiajun faltered. He slipped and bumped into Ahn Hyun Soo, who had started to move in on Apolo's inside. Ahn Hyun Soo was suddenly tumbling through the air. The next person to fall was Apolo, followed by Li Jiajun, and then Canada's Mathieu Turcotte. Four of the best 1,000-meter short track speed skaters were suddenly skidding into the padded boards at the side of the rink.

Only one skater was still standing: Steven Bradbury of Australia. He had been skating in last place and so had avoided the accident. In the next instant he was across the finish line. He had taken the gold.

The crowd was stunned. They were there to see Apolo win. And he had been winning. He should have taken first. Instead, he was tangled in a pile of spandex and helmets and razor-sharp skates.

There was total confusion.

But there was one person who wasn't confused: Apolo. He was only thinking about the race and the finish line. The race may have seemed over to the audience, but Apolo knew it wasn't. Gold was gone, but there were two medals left to claim.

In the next second he was on his feet. The finish line was only meters away. He staggered toward the line, half skating, half crawling. The other three racers saw what was happening and started scrambling toward the line themselves. But Apolo had the jump on them. In the next second, he was over the line and had taken second. Next across was Mathieu Turcotte, who wasn't even skating—he was crawling. He claimed the bronze. Li Jiajun and Ahn Hyun Soo could only watch in disbelief as they, too, tried to scramble forward. But it was too late. They had been denied a medal.

The crowd watched in confusion and disbelief. They couldn't process what had happened. Short track speed skating is a new sport. People knew who Apolo was but weren't really sure how the short track worked.

Suddenly the fans became furious. They had watched Apolo hold the lead for most of the race. He had been in first place only meters before the finish line. They thought he should have won. They definitely didn't think that the guy holding last place should be walking away with the gold. They thought there should be a do-over. The crowd booed and hissed and chanted "U-S-A."

But the race was over. That was short track. It's a gutsy sport where races often end with crashes. That's what's great about it. It's what Apolo loves about it. And he wasn't crying foul. The race had been clean, despite the crashes, and Apolo was ready to take the breaks as they came.

In fact, Apolo was clearly happy. Really happy. He smiled as he skated off the ice. He had won a silver medal in the Olympics. That was reason enough for him to feel good about the night.

It had been a great race with a spectacular ending. It was the sort of thing that Apolo loved about his sport. And he was kind of proud of himself. Quick decision making and a burst of energy at the end had got him a silver medal. It could have been a lot worse.

But Apolo's smiles and laughter were also surprising for another reason. They were surprising because he had been pretty banged up in the crash, and he was bleeding all over his spandex suit. He had slashed himself on the inside of his left thigh with his own skate. It was a potentially serious injury. In fact, Steven Bradbury, the gold medal winner, had almost died from a similar injury a few years earlier, having lost over half his blood on the ice.

Doctors rushed to Apolo and started bandaging him up. But Apolo was still all smiles. In fact, he could barely contain his joy. And when he made it onto the podium later on, he was still smiling and laughing. They had to bring him over to the podium in a wheelchair, and he barely managed to stagger up to the silver pedestal. But he was enjoying every minute of it. He even hugged Steven Bradbury when Steven was given the gold. It had been a great race, and Apolo was happy to have been in it. He didn't feel even a shred of disappointment.

Apolo was beginning to distinguish himself again. He was one of the best short track speed skaters in the world. Everyone knew that. What they didn't know was what a good sport he was. The story of the kid who hung out with gangs, stayed out all night, and ate Pizza Hut at training camp had just gotten much, much better.

Apolo hadn't just become a great skater. He had also become a great competitor. The crowd that had just been booing the race because Apolo had been denied the gold was now cheering. Apolo was thrilled. Why shouldn't they be? Apolo had an Olympic medal. And he had really earned it. He had skated a great race. Everyone was celebrating—Apolo, the coaches, the fans, and especially Mr. Ohno.

But now the race was over. Apolo had new things to think about. There were still three events ahead, and despite his happiness, something else was on Apolo's mind: his leg. It was a potentially serious injury, especially since he had a week and a half of races ahead of him.

He wasn't sure what would happen in the next events. Would he be able to do his best?

Would he even be able to compete?

First Gold

The day after the 1,000-meter crash, sports page headlines were all telling of the crazy day on the short track. And when Apolo showed up at the press conference, it was all anyone wanted to talk about.

The first reason they were interested was because Apolo had shown up on crutches. The press was obviously thrown by this. Apolo was one of the heroes of the games. He had three more finals. What did the crutches mean? Was Apolo out of it already?

Apolo assured people that he was not out. He wasn't sure how his injury would affect him, but he wasn't giving up. He had six stitches beneath the bandages. He was sore. But his muscle had not been punctured. It could have been a lot worse. It might hurt a little to skate, but pain was part of the sport. His plan was to take the coming Sunday off to heal and then get back on the ice on Monday.

After Apolo's health was discussed, the press moved to the other issue—his silver medal. Again, Apolo could not have been happier. He took the whole thing like a true sportsman.

"This was the best race of my life," he told the press. "I skated it exactly like I wanted. Unfortunately I went down in the last corner. But this is the sport I train for. I got the silver medal, so I can't complain."

He was also full of praise for the gold medalist, Steven Bradbury. Steven had been in three Olympics but had never won before. He had paid his dues. He had devoted his life to the sport. He had even broken his neck during a training session a year and a half earlier. This guy had gone through a lot to be at Salt Lake City. Apolo was happy to see that kind of struggle rewarded. Steven had become the first Australian ever to win a gold medal in the Winter Olympic games.

The two were also pretty good friends. Steven runs a company in Australia that makes skates, including the skates that Apolo wears.

Steven and Apolo had e-mailed back and forth the night before the race. Steven had asked Apolo to put in a good word about his company when he was on the podium. The two had had no idea how the race would really turn out. Now that Steven had won a gold medal, he'd have the chance to pitch his company himself. Apolo was very happy about that.

The press conference ended with a little more drama. Apolo had arrived on crutches, but that wasn't the way he left. Doctors wanted Apolo to take it easy, so they brought in a wheelchair. In the next instant he was being wheeled out of the room.

Just a precaution, the press was told. Still, people were left wondering.

On Monday, everyone's questions about Apolo's health were finally answered. He was back on the ice, training, and he looked great. When asked about the practice afterward he said, "I had pain, but I always feel pain. That's part of the sport."

He wasn't back to normal, but he was close. And he still had Tuesday to recover. The next event was the 1,500-meter, on Wednesday. He'd have to make it through two heats before the final, so there would be three races in all.

--·--

No one thought the injury would be a problem. As the team doctor said, "He's a pretty motivated guy. Once the gun goes off, he won't even think about it."

In fact, the whole coaching staff seemed pretty optimistic. They all knew Apolo and were more than impressed by his burning drive to compete. They shrugged off the crash and the injury as no big deal. As Susan Ellis, the head coach for the short track squad, said: "If you don't want to occasionally crash into the boards and lose, then you shouldn't do short track. Just like if you don't want to maybe fall down real hard and break a leg, you don't do the downhill. Those are the risks."

Obviously, short track is not a good sport if you want a lot of pampering and sympathy from your coach.

The other thing Apolo had going for him was the length of the next race. It was 1,500 meters. Because this race is the longest of the short track events, skaters have to take it more slowly. It's not just a mad-dash sprint like the 500. Skaters don't need the same lightning burst of quick power to win. Pacing is what counts.

Apolo wouldn't need to go crazy off the starting line. He could move into the race more easily. That would help his injured leg.

When Wednesday came, Apolo looked ready. He lined up for the first two heats and blew through them, no problem. He was expected to get into the final, and he did. The cut to his left thigh didn't seem to factor in at all. Still, even if he weren't injured, winning the final would be hard.

Once again, the Delta Center was packed. But the fans were a little more experienced now, a little more knowledgeable.

First, everyone knew about the crash. Speed skating was suddenly the most exciting, high-drama sport in the Olympics. If the first race was that exciting, fans couldn't wait to see what the next one brought.

People were now also completely familiar with Apolo's story. They knew about his past, what he had done to get to the Olympics, how he'd been injured, and how well he'd taken the 1,000-meter defeat. Apolo was no longer the kid with potential. He was a seasoned Olympic medalist and a bona fide hero.

Of course, not everyone was there to cheer for Apolo. There were fans from all over the world, many of whom had their own favorites. But most people there were rooting for Apolo. If there was any doubt about Apolo's draw, all you had to do was look around the arena. Not only were there signs everywhere, but people had figured out another way to honor the new golden boy of the Olympics. Mimicking the little tuft of hair that Apolo had growing from his chin (something the press was calling a "soul patch") people had taped false beards, black tape, and stickers onto their chins. It was Apolo's night, and people were there to celebrate him, beard and all.

By the time he lined up for the final, the crowd was bringing down the roof. Chants of "Apolo" and "U-S-A" filled the Delta Center.

Next to Apolo, four other racers took their positions. There were Li Jiajun of China, Marc Gagnon of Canada, Fabio Carta of Italy, and Kim Dong Sung of South Korea. Each was a star in his own right, and each was ready to fight to bring gold back to his country.

The 1,500-meter had four and a half more laps than the 1,000-meter, so the start was not as crucial. Still this race was going to be over in about two and a half minutes, so a good start would be a big help.

The five racers took their marks and prepared for the gun. Once again, Apolo slipped into his trance state, and the focus set in.

There was a finish line. It was 1,500 meters away. He had to get there first.

It was that simple.

Bang. The gun sounded and the racers were off.

Once again, short track speed skating is about strategy as much as speed. There was no advantage to Apolo taking an early lead. He had explosive power. It was just a matter of timing. He had to wait until the right moment. The lead only counted at the finish line, and in the first laps, Apolo stayed at the back of the pack.

The crowd was going crazy. The skaters were flying around the ice, touching it with their hands as they rounded the curves. People were continuing to chant, waving their banners and rubbing their phony soul patches for luck. Tonight was Apolo's night to claim gold. He had been denied it four nights ago. This was his night.

Apolo continued to hold the rear. He wasn't moving early, but by the middle of the race he wasn't charging forward either. He was still at the back.

No one knew what was up. It could be his injured leg. It could just be an off night.

Or maybe Apolo had a plan.

What Apolo was doing was waiting. He had been doing this for years. It was all about waiting for the right time to make your move. But he was waiting a long time, and with three laps left, people were starting to get nervous.

Finally, with two laps to go, Apolo gunned it.

In a few seconds Apolo moved past three people. He had gone from last place to second place, and he was coming in hard on South Korean Kim Dong Sung, who held the lead. Even though Apolo was in second, it looked like he was going to win. Apolo was moving so quickly that there was almost nothing that could stop him. He was going much faster than Kim Dong Sung. People could see his incredible speed and judge it against the distance to the finish line.

He was going to do it. Apolo was going to take the gold.

But suddenly, as Apolo came up on the inside of Kim Dong Sung, the South Korean cut to his side, blocking Apolo. Apolo almost crashed into him and had to quickly pull up and lift his arms to avoid a crash. He was almost knocked over.

Apolo looked shaken and surprised.

What Kim Dong Sung had done is called cross-tracking, and in the sport of short track, it's illegal. You are not allowed to block someone's track. If they are skating faster, you have to let them by. Apolo might have been able to readjust. He might have been able to make another move. But it was too late. Kim Dong Sung had cross-tracked in the final turn.

In another second, they were over the finish line. Kim Dong Sung had snatched the gold.

Apolo once again had placed second. Another silver. Had he been robbed?

The crowd certainly seemed to think so. They were furious. Enough people there understood the rules of short track to know that what Kim Dong Sung had done was illegal. It was Apolo's race, and it had been taken from him.

Just four nights earlier he had lost gold under unfortunate circumstances. Now it was happening again.

Kim Dong Sung was uninterested in the

crowd's reaction. He had been given a huge South Korean flag from someone in the audience and was taking his victory lap. He held the flag above him and was celebrating his victory.

Apolo was confused, but he was taking it well. He understood that his sport was full of tough breaks. Sometimes things went your way, sometimes they didn't. Still, this was a hard pill to swallow. Apolo had just lost his second gold.

Then suddenly there was a commotion among the referees. They were conferring and then signaling to the scorekeeper. Apolo wasn't paying attention. He was thinking about the race. Suddenly he heard an enormous burst of applause from the crowd and looked up at the scoreboard. Kim Dong Sung had been disqualified for his cross-tracking. Apolo had won the gold.

It was an incredible moment. There on the ice, two opposite emotions were suddenly apparent. The Korean fans were overcome with disappointment. Kim Dong Sung sadly dropped his flag. It was a tough blow, but something that often happens in short track racing. Kim Dong Sung had gone from gold to disqualification. It was a hard thing for him to take.

And then there was Apolo.

He had gone from silver to gold in a single, strange instant. He was suddenly in the middle of the ice smiling and laughing, holding his hands in the air. He was in disbelief. In another minute he was down on his knees, unable to think about what was going on.

The crowd was reacting the same way. Within the space of a few seconds, they had suffered massive disappointment and then stunning joy. Their hero had lost the gold that he had worked so long to achieve. And then it had been returned to him.

The U.S. coaches reacted this way as well. They had been working with Apolo for a long time. They had seen him in the days when he was blowing off practice for Pizza Hut. And they had seen him when he was training like a maniac and winning everything. They had seen all the agony and all the hard work.

This was the ultimate payoff.

And there was one other guy who was pretty happy—probably the man who'd had to put up with the most over the years—Mr. Ohno. His reaction was a little steadier but also a little more emotional. He was doing all he could to stop the tears coming to his eyes. All the work and all the worry with this kid who used to eat rocks and escape from day care had paid off. Apolo had seen some bad days and had been tempted by some bad things, but now everything was all right. Everything had finally worked out.

He had won an Olympic gold medal.

In the interviews right after the victory, Apolo was almost incomprehensible. He was exhausted and thrilled and giddy with excitement. He was gasping for breath and bewildered by all the camera flashes and all the chanting. He could only laugh and say how happy he was.

"I just feel so good," he said. "I come here, perform my best, and get a gold medal. There's nothing better than that."

Then, after a few more questions, it was off the ice to await the medal ceremony. And when that came, the fanfare started all over again. As Apolo received the gold, and the American flag was hoisted above the arena, and the national anthem was played, everything was finally in harmony. The gold was his. He had earned it. The fans at the stadium and the fans watching their televisions were delirious. He was a true Olympic champ.

And the night brought more celebrating. Apolo says that he didn't get to sleep till 4 A.M. that night. He was too excited, too pumped up. It was impossible to rest. And the coaching staff and Apolo's father felt the same way. Everyone was too excited to relax.

The next morning was the same, but a new issue had come up. People were starting to ask whether Kim Dong Sung's disqualification had been a fair call. Some people were wondering if the gold should really be Apolo's.

In some ways, Kim Dong Sung's disqualification raised questions that are a central issue of short track. Technically, skaters are never supposed to bump or jostle anyone, and they're not supposed to block each other either. But it happens. Sometimes it gets called, sometimes it doesn't. In the case of Kim Dong Sung, some people thought that the judges were being too tough. Others thought that the call was right on. Really, it's no different than any sport. There is chance involved, and any given day can bring sudden defeat and stunning victory depending on how the refs call the race.

Because there is some chance involved, however, people often question calls to make sure the judging was fair. The day after the race, the South Korean Olympic Committee and the South Korean media wanted the disqualification reviewed.

And other people shared their opinions. Right after the race, the Italian racer, Fabio Carta, said that it wasn't the right call and that Kim Dong Sung shouldn't have been disqualified. Other skaters agreed with him.

On the other hand, there were plenty of onlookers who supported the call and thought Apolo deserved the gold. Dutch skater Cees Juffermans told the *Washington Post* that "the moment Kim made the move, I knew it was over. It was definitely cross-track."

It was a tough question, but trying to figure out how to apply the rules of a sport is what the Olympics are all about. People work hard to be there, and everyone wants to make sure that judging is fair and consistent.

Perhaps one of the best perspectives on the issue came from Apolo himself. When the gold came his way, he shrugged his shoulders and took the whole thing calmly. He agreed with the call. He claimed that Kim definitely came over on him and that his disqualification was a good, fair judgment. But he never got angry and he never got defensive. He behaved just as he had when he'd won the silver.

Sometimes calls go your way, sometimes they don't. Apolo never did anything but smile and laugh about the whole thing. He just calmly let the discussion go on around him without paying too much attention. As he said in one press conference when asked about Kim Dong Sung's disqualification, "That's not really my focus. My concentration, my main focus, is on the 500-meter [on] Saturday."

The discussion over Kim Dong Sung's disqualification eventually died down, and the Korean Olympic Committee came to terms with the loss. The International Olympic Committee considered the South Korean's request to review the call, but in the end decided that the referee's judgment is final in this kind of situation. The South Korean squad lived with the ruling and moved on.

And the fact was that the Olympics were far from over. South Korea had a fantastic team, and there were still two more short track events left. Everyone was trying to put the disqualification behind them. People wanted to stay on target. Again, distraction is the enemy of any short track skater.

The skaters needed things to get back to normal as quickly as possible.

CHAPTER NINE

The End of the Ride

Two more races, two more chances to medal. Apolo was thrilled with his performances so far. He could walk away happy.

But you don't get as far as Apolo has without wanting to win it all. Apolo was there for four events, and he was going to do what he could to win the final two.

The remaining races were the 500-meter and the 5,000-meter relay. They were both on the final night of the Olympics: Saturday, February 23.

It was probably the most exciting night of the games. The atmosphere of the Delta Center was more like that of a carnival than a sporting event.

A lot of other events were over, and athletes

could blow off some steam without worrying about their next race. Many had come to the arena to check out the short track. They wanted to see what all the talk was about. And they wanted to relax and have fun.

One of Apolo's biggest fans happened to be another Olympic athlete—Michelle Kwan, the bronze medal winner in women's figure skating. She was there to cheer on Apolo, and she had even brought a sign. It had a drawing of a pair of lips saying "Oh yes, Ohno."

There were other famous visitors as well. Movie stars and billionaires had come to see the last night of short track competition. Even former New York mayor Rudolph Giuliani was there to check out Apolo's stuff.

But as usual, it was the anonymous fans who made the night so great. People who had no real experience with winter sports had suddenly become short track addicts. There were also people there who didn't necessarily love short track, but who definitely loved Apolo. And then there were the die-hard fans who had been watching from the beginning, holding up signs and wearing fake beards to cheer Apolo on. Someone even put a fake beard on his dog to honor the nineteen-year-old from

Seattle. And there were also the people who knew nothing about short track speed skating and didn't know any of the skaters. They, too, were having the time of their lives. The mood was so giddy and exciting. Who wouldn't have fun?

Apolo was definitely there to have fun.

But he was also there to win.

The 500-meter was going to be a tough race for Apolo. It's an event that depends on how quickly a skater can get off the line. Apolo's leg was a lot better. The cut was healing. But he was still injured. In a sport where inches separate first and second place, it could be the deciding factor.

But Apolo was skating well that night. He made it to the semifinals, blowing by opponent after opponent. It looked like it was going to be a repeat of Wednesday night. He had a real shot of going all the way and taking gold.

When Apolo lined up for the semis, the crowd again disappeared from his mind. He was conscious only of the ice and his opponents. Suddenly the gun sounded and the skaters were sprinting forward.

Unfortunately, Apolo didn't get off the mark as quickly as he had wanted to. It wasn't anything to worry about. Apolo was great at coming up with last-minute bursts of speed. Still, because it was such a short race, it would have been nice if he had gotten the jump on his opponents.

Apolo was still in it, though. Everyone knew that this kid was the biggest threat out there. He stayed near the back of the pack, biding his time. It was a similar strategy to the one he had used in the 1,500-meter—hang back and wait for the opportunity to strike.

Finally, the chance came. Apolo was in third place as he began his charge to the front. There was a hole up ahead. There wasn't much time left. He had to take the chance.

He powered ahead, leaning into the turn, preparing to squeeze through. The hole was on the inside of the skater just ahead of him—a guy named Satoru Terao, from Japan. He paused, sized up his position, and then burst forward, trying to edge past Satoru Terao.

But he couldn't quite make it. There wasn't enough space. Instead, speeding along at thirty-five miles per hour, he bumped into Terao. The Japanese skater lurched forward, spun out of control, and went crashing to the side of the ice.

Apolo was skating too aggressively. It was an accident. It was nothing unusual on the short track. Still, Apolo had to pay the consequences for the mistake. As he crossed the finish line, he saw that he had been disqualified. His spot in the finals was awarded to Satoru Terao.

Those were the breaks. Apolo knew it. He didn't dispute the call. Just as he had in the last two events, he recognized that this was just the way that short track worked.

Apolo smiled as he headed off the ice. He was disappointed, but he wasn't angry. As he said later on, in his usual relaxed and philosophical tone, "I got a little too anxious. The contact was incidental. I was waiting for the opportunity. I ran up on him, and he went down." And then he added, "But that's all right—I've still got the relay." In typical Apolo fashion, he just dealt with his defeat and started thinking about the next race.

But this isn't to say that Apolo lost all interest in the 500-meter. His buddy Rusty Smith had qualified and was going to be in the final. Amazingly, Rusty came in third. He won a bronze, his first medal of the games. If Apolo couldn't win a medal, the next best thing was a friend winning one. Apolo was overjoyed.

Now it was time to regroup. The team had to get ready for the relay.

The team consisted of Apolo, Rusty, a skater named Daniel Weinstein, and Ron Biondo. Fortunately, Ron, Apolo, and Rusty had patched up their differences from the earlier Olympic trials. They were ready to work together. And with Apolo skating, it looked like this might be gold for team USA.

The race started well. But a lot can happen in 5,000 meters. There was no reason to be too hopeful.

The one thing for sure was that the U.S. was skating a good race—exactly the race they wanted to skate. They quickly established themselves in second place, an ideal spot for a long race. First place has to put up with wind resistance. The second skater can ride right behind the first, going the same speed but not expending the same energy because of the diminished force of the wind.

The other great thing about second was that it set the Americans up for a big move. They weren't so off the lead that they couldn't speed ahead to first.

Everything was going well. The crowd was cheering. Michelle Kwan was waving her banner. Mr. Ohno was standing and clapping. People were chanting "U-S-A, U-S-A."

Suddenly, disaster struck.

It was lap twenty-six. Rusty Smith had the baton. He was getting ready to pass it off to Ron. He took a tight turn, gauging the opponent ahead of him. Suddenly, his skate caught one of the black rubber markers that outlines the track. He was up in the air and hurtling toward the ice. In the next instant he was on his back and spinning toward the padded boards at the side of the rink.

He was dazed but then suddenly figured out what had happened. It was a forty-five-lap race. There were still nineteen laps to go. Rusty got back up and kept going. He lurched forward and passed the baton off to Ron. Ron took the baton and started his charge. But it was too late. The gap was too big.

Team USA would never catch up. They had lost. No medals for the relay team.

As he sat in the press conference afterward, Rusty could only apologize. No one held it against him, especially not his teammates. Again, this was the kind of thing that happened in short track speed skating. But Rusty was disappointed. They'd had a shot at gold. It was just unfortunate that such a small misstep had cost them the race.

Apolo was relaxed after the race. It was disappointing, but again, it was all part of the sport he loved. Talking about all the insane finishes in the short track events, he just smiled and shrugged his shoulders as he always did.

It just seemed to be the way his whole Olympics had turned out. Between all he had done to get to Salt Lake, all the crashes and disqualifications while he was there, the injuries, and the flu, the relay race didn't seem any different than everything else that had happened. He just said, "Lots of crazy things happen in the Olympics. You ask any athlete: If something crazy is going to happen, it's going to happen here."

And the fact was that Apolo had done pretty well—probably better than most athletes can even hope for. As he said: "I got a silver medal and a gold medal and another two awesome performances, so this is definitely the highlight of my career."

But the more reflective Apolo also had this to add when someone asked about his Olympic experience: "My journey is not about winning medals. It's about being able to go to the starting line in the Olympics, experiencing it and performing at my best. Things like that happen in this sport. It's what I live for. I was happy with my performance."

Apolo had proved many things at the 2002 Salt Lake Olympics. One was that he was one of the best short track speed skaters in the world. But that was something everyone already knew.

More important, he proved what a kind, generous, and gracious athlete he is. Not everyone expected this from the kid who used to hang out with gangs and blow off practices.

After the Olympics, everyone knew that Apolo was a true Olympic champion—something it takes more than just medals to become.

Chapter Ten:

New Inspiration

So what was next for Apolo? As he watched the fireworks exploding above him at the Olympics' closing ceremonies, this was exactly the question that was on his mind.

Just what *was* next?

For lots of people, it would have been a good time to hang up the skates and try something new. Apolo had signed a deal with Nike, and his agents had set up a huge list of other companies that wanted a piece of this hip young gold medalist. That meant a lot of money. It meant that Apolo would be even more of a star.

So why not take a break, relax, and start enjoying the profits of all that hard labor? He'd paid his dues. Maybe this was the time to goof around on the Washington coast, party in LA with other celebs, or hit swanky restaurants in New York City.

The fact is, you don't get to be the best speed skater in the world unless you love your sport, and Apolo loves the short track more than anything else. For Apolo, the ultimate reward, the ultimate payoff, is the competition itself. And in the midst of the movie stars and cheering fans who swarmed the closing ceremonies at Rice-Eccles Olympic Stadium, Apolo realized that the reason he was there was not the glitz and glam. It was because he loved the ice. He loved to compete. And as the fanfare swirled around him, he was ecstatic. He had come to the 2002 Games and given the best performances of his life. That was all he wanted. That was why he was so happy.

He also knew he had a lot of skating ahead of him. Apolo is at the height of his career. He only seems to be getting better. And he's still very young. Most skaters don't peak until their midtwenties. Apolo probably has another ten good years of blowing by opponents, crashing into the boards, dodging rink markers, and lurching over the finish line. There's not much in the world that excites Apolo more than that.

In fact, the thing on his mind now is the next Olympics. They'll be in Turin, Italy, in 2006. Apolo will be twenty-three—still young for a short track skater. Four more gold medals will be up for grabs in Turin.

For a guy like Apolo, all the parties in Hollywood can't match the fun of competing for those.

Still, just because he's going to keep skating doesn't mean he's not going to have some fun along the way. He's already been completely booked on the talk show circuit. He's been on *The Conan O'Brien Show* and *The Tonight Show with Jay Leno*. He's been on the *Today Show* a few times. (He taught Katie Couric how to skate, and the *Today Show* fans even voted Apolo as the "Athlete who most embodies the Olympic spirit.") And when he showed up for *The Rosie O'Donnell Show*, Rosie even gave him a brand-new car. Apolo had no idea it was coming. He had shown up to give a brief interview, but Rosie liked him so much and thought he had worked so hard that she gave him a brand-new Pontiac Aztec! Apolo was totally shocked.

Apolo has also been on MTV. He was a special guest on *Total Request Live*, where he showed off some of his breakdancing moves. People were absolutely stunned. Fans knew that Apolo was a good athlete, but his dazzling acrobatic dance moves surprised everyone, especially the studio audience. They were so blown away they didn't even know how to react.

So with all the talk shows and free cars and appearances on MTV, Apolo looks like he's got some good times ahead of him. With the Nike deal and the other ad deals on their way, he's going to be well taken care of for the rest of his life. And he's earned it.

This kid with the powerful legs and big heart worked hard for the attention he's now getting, and most people couldn't be happier for a guy who has as much personality and grace as Apolo does.

But Apolo's achievements are also important in a way beyond the things he's earned for himself. Probably the biggest winner from the 2002 Olympics has been short track speed skating itself.

Before Salt Lake City, people weren't quite sure what to make of this strange new sport. Some compared it to roller derby. Others thought the crashes and contact made it seem more like ice hockey than racing. There were the die-hard fans, of course. But they were few and far between. Mostly it was the kind of sport that was never on television, rarely covered in newspapers, and wasn't even a big deal at the Olympics.

But just like a movie gets a lift from having a big star play the lead, short track came alive as people began to learn more about Apolo. They read about his background, heard interviews with his father, and wondered what to make of such an unusual story. Kids saw the guy with the little beard on his chin and the bandana and the earring, and decided they could relate to him. And once the Olympics finally began, people started tuning in when short track was on. They kept up with the news, followed the scores, and watched as the subject of the story they had fallen in love with proceeded to prove he was one of the best in the world.

And the momentum grew. After the crash in the 1,000-meter, people wanted to know more about the kid who had scrapped his way to a silver and was so gracious in defeat. They wanted to see the guy who won the gold after Kim Dong Sung had been disqualified. People wanted to know more about the guy with long hair who was always on the *Today Show* and late-night TV.

And in learning more about Apolo, people fell in love with the short track. Fans tuned in again and again, making short track speed skating one of the most popular sports in the Winter Olympics.

It's hard to say what will happen next with short track. But it's definitely here to stay. With as many new fans as the 2002 Olympics brought in, there'd be a riot if the sport were dropped in 2006.

And Apolo probably coaxed a few young skaters into giving the short track a shot. A bunch of kids saw short track on television for the first time in 2002 just like Apolo did in 1994. Maybe some won't be interested. But you can bet a few will be. They'll probably even be getting a new pair of skates when the next Christmas or birthday or Hanukah rolls around—just like Apolo did.

A whole new generation of short track skaters will be born, and Apolo will have been their inspiration.

Quick Facts About Apolo

HEIGHT: 5' 7"
WEIGHT: 165 pounds
BIRTHDAY: May 22, 1982
HOMETOWN: Seattle, Washington
CURRENT RESIDENCE: Colorado Springs, Colorado
SPORT: Short Track Speed Skating
TEAM: U.S. Elite Short Track Team
FAVORITE BOOK: *Way of the Peaceful Warrior* by Dan Millman
FAVORITE MUSIC: Hip hop, rhythm and blues
INTERESTS: Hanging out with friends, dancing, music, basketball

Apolo Ohno
Competitive History

Gold, 1,500-meter, 2002 Olympics
Silver, 1,000-meter, 2002 Olympics
World Record, 1,500 meters:
Kearns, Utah, 1 min., 27.41 seconds
U.S. National Champion, 2002
World Cup Overall Champion, 2001
World Cup Champion 500-meter, 2001
World Cup Champion 1,000-meter, 2001
World Cup Champion 1,500-meter, 2001
U.S. National Champion, 2001
U.S. Junior Short Track Overall Champion, 2000
Winner, Junior World Championships, 1999
U.S. National Champion, 1999
Silver, 500-meter, 1999 World Championship
U.S. National Champion, 1997*

*At 14, youngest ever to win U.S. National Championships

History of Olympic Short Track Speed Skating

500-METER

SALT LAKE CITY 2002

Gold	Marc Gagnon	Canada
Silver	Jonathan Guilmette	Canada
Bronze	Rusty Smith	US

NAGANO 1998

Gold	Takafumi Nishitani	Japan
Silver	An Yulong	China
Bronze	Hitoshi Uematsu	Japan

LILLEHAMMER 1994

Gold	Chae Ji Hoon	South Korea
Silver	Mirko Vuillermin	Italy
Bronze	Nicholas Gooch	Great Britain

1,000-METER

Salt Lake City 2002

Gold	Steven Bradbury	Australia
Silver	Apolo Anton Ohno	United States
Bronze	Mathieu Turcotte	Canada

Nagano 1998

Gold	Kim Dong Sung	South Korea
Silver	Li Jaijun	China
Bronze	Eric Bedard	Canada

Lillehammer 1994

Gold	Ki-Hoon Kim	South Korea
Silver	Chae Ji Hoon	South Korea
Bronze	Marc Gagnon	Canada

Albertville 1992

Gold	Ki-Hoon Kim	South Korea
Silver	Frederic Blackburn	Canada
Bronze	Joon-Ho Lee	South Korea

1,500-METER

SALT LAKE CITY 2002
Gold	Apolo Anton Ohno	United States
Silver	Li Jiajun	China
Bronze	Marc Gagnon	Canada

5,000-METER RELAY

SALT LAKE CITY 2002
Gold	Canada
Silver	Italy
Bronze	China

NAGANO 1998
Gold	Canada
Silver	South Korea
Bronze	China

LILLEHAMMER 1994
Gold	Italy
Silver	United States and Australia (TIE)

ALBERTVILLE 1992
Gold	Korea
Silver	Canada
Bronze	Japan

Photo Credits